Making Dollars Make $ense:
Business Ownership at any Age

CHEURLIE PIERRE-RUSSELL

BOOKS BY C. PIERRE-RUSSELL

Sheila the Shy Shark

Save the Missing Penny

The Beauty of Love in Those We Shame

Little Kitty Goes to School

Broken before the Storm

The Special Little Sister

The Better Betty

Friendly Monsters: Behind the Computer

Making Dollars Make $ense: Business Ownership at any Age

Butter Me Fly: My Way Home

Publishing Information

Printed in the United States of America

All rights reserved. Except as permitted under the U.S. Copyright Act of 1976, no part of this publication may be reproduced, distributed or transmitted in any form or by any means, or stored in a database or retrieval system, without the prior written permission of the publisher.

This is a work of nonfiction. The story is told with the express permission of the real characters whose names are protected for confidentiality.

Any other resemblance to actual persons, living or dead, business establishments, events or locales is entirely coincidental and incidental to the real events in the time period the story is placed.

Copyright © 2018 Cheurlie Pierre-Russell,
Miami, Florida.
All Rights Reserved

Introduction

We've all read those news stories about the young kid who set up a business and made a whole heap of cash, right? Well, that kid was nothing special. Believe me—he or she is just like you.

That kid just decided to be an entrepreneur and committed his efforts to it; he or she made a big decision very early in life, to earn money—and to earn it like crazy—letting nothing get in the way.

The more you believe in yourself—and in choosing what you love to do—the better you can be as a business kid or *entrepreneur*.

Money, money, and more money can be made by just about anyone, especially children like you. I have you guessing how can it happen, right?

First, think about that one special thing you love to do. Or find out what kind of talent you have at school and at home.

Everyone is talented at something they enjoy doing. Finding the *something* that you especially enjoy doing will only encourage you to continue doing it. And people who keep on doing and doing the something that they love, become really, really good at it—and being really, really good at something can earn a lot of money.

People who become moguls do exactly that; it's not rocket science, is it? These people, including business kids the world over, simply make money doing something they enjoy doing, something they're passionate about. They don't look at their job like it's just a job—because they enjoy doing it.

So, it feels more a hobby or a pastime than a job. When you love your hobby, you will do it long-term to reach your goal. Remember, you do not want to make it feel like a job when you get into it. It will be something you love doing while benefiting from it and making money in a fun way. So, you have the power to start your very own business and be that boss girl or boy you were born to be. In the next few pages, you will discover simple business ideas you can practice and begin to earn your first dollars, with no stress.

Selling Candy

Think about how you can you earn money every day rather than ask anyone for any handouts. Imagine getting to a stage where you can take or leave your pocket money, because you earn more by standing on your own two feet doing what you love to do!

Every kid knows it can become aggravating to ask your parents for money every day, especially when you want to go off to the movies or bowling with your friends. The kids are ready to go, and you're still trying to find that $1 coin that was rolling around your pocket among all the candy wrappers a week ago!

If your parents do not have any money—or they just don't think you should have any from them *today*—then guess what, you won't be able to go unless you find that $1, and even that won't go far!

Therefore, to become a mogul kid, you need to think wise and be willing to learn how to double or triple your own money to make it grow. Instead of just taking that shiny new $1 from your parents, think about how to hold onto it a few days and turn it into a few dollars, or you can think even bigger and start something from scratch; many small business ideas don't even need any start-up capital! (*Capital* is the money used to create a new business).

Other small business ideas might need a bit more money at the start, and here's where you'll hit the jackpot if you have the sort of parents who'll join you in backing your idea and putting in that initial investment of cash for you to get going. If you want to impress them, why not even write out a Start-Up Contract on a piece of paper?

Here's an example! It doesn't need to be anything difficult.

'I, Adam Smith of (ADDRESS) undertake to use the sum of $(ENTER $ SUM) received from (PARENTS' NAMES) to start up my business (ENTER NAME OF BUSINESS) and for no other purpose.

With this borrowed sum, I will (TELL THEM WHAT YOU'LL USE IT FOR, e.g., 'buy stock/set up a stall/buy a bicycle to run my errands/buy typing paper so I can deliver flyers around the neighborhood' etc.)

I hereby undertake to give my parents back their (ENTER SUM BORROWED) as soon as I can, from my earnings.'

Signed: (Your signature).

Dated: (Today's date).

You could even add:

'I will hold a meeting with my parents on (DATE) to show how my business is going and to invite feedback.'

See how that shows your parents how responsible and businesslike you plan to be? And not just that, but it also tells them they will get their money back if you earn from your venture! And it shows them a lot of thought is going into your new business idea; you're not just asking for a handout to go and waste on something. Even better, you are not going to disappear with the cash; you are already inviting them along to a business meeting to report on your progress!

When you schedule your first business meeting with your parents, don't do it too soon, yet soon enough that it keeps you driving toward your goal. You could schedule it in two weeks or four weeks' time, depending on what you have to do to get the business going. You won't necessarily need to have made sales already when the meeting happens; this is about showing where their cash was invested and what your plans are to take the business forward.

What sort of money might you ask them for?

Well, that depends on what your business model is. A *business model* really just means, what the business is all about and how you'll run it. So, for example, business models to sell candy or walk the neighbors' dogs are simpler and cheaper models than to create original artwork or to do garden remodeling, or to run a bicycle courier service, because in the last three examples, you may need to buy some expensive stock (paints and crayons, brushes, easels, a bicycle, gardening tools, etc.,) to get going unless your parents already have what you'll need.

Children Business Model

Your business name: _____
Your chosen business idea: _____
Who will you sell to: _____
Do you need any money to get started? _____
If so, how much do you need? _____
How much will you charge? _____
How much will you make from each sale? _____

WHAT YOU NEED TO DO WITH THE MONEY YOU MAKE?

* Use some to buy more supplies
* Put the rest in a Piggy Bank

So, let's start by thinking of the candy-selling business model:

You can ask your parents for $20 only once and start your own business right away. Take the $20 and buy one or two boxes of candy.

STOP! Put those sticky little fingers away! DO NOT EAT THE CANDY! This is what most kids would do—and in fact, most grown-ups would too! But remember, this is your business and the $20 you just used when you bought the candy is not even yours.

Remember why?

It's because you borrowed it—which means you must not eat that candy yourself or you can't pay the money back because you'll have eaten all the stock you were going to sell. Hmm, if you have a sweet tooth, maybe candy is not your winning business idea! ☺

But for now, let's assume that you are not going to eat all that candy and that you're safe to buy it for resale. You can buy your stock—the candies you'll resell—from a store or you can be even cleverer and go online to seek out cheaper outlets. Buying online means you can get stock at a fraction of what it will sell for in the mall—and lower buying prices mean a lot more profit—the money you'll make—for you.

And even when you're shopping for that candy online, don't just take the first stockiest you find; put the name of the candy into Google and see what other stockists come up, as you may just find it cheaper somewhere else. Remember to look, too, at what it costs to have it shipped to you and how long it will take to reach you, because in business, 'time is money'! While you're waiting for the candies to arrive, you could be losing profits, so try and find the seller who gives a good price—even if not the cheapest—plus a good shipping price, and a reasonable delivery time. You can't expect them to do great at everything, so decide what's most important and stick to that seller. Oh, and check out their reviews to see they're a really good seller!

So, now your candies have arrived, here's what to do next.

Find out the usual price of a box of that candy—not the cheapest price you bought the box for, but what you'd usually have to pay for one full box—and count how many candies come in the box. With these pieces of information, you will know how much profit you'll make. (A recap: a profit is the extra money that you made when you subtract the amount of money you spent from the amount of candies sold. In arithmetic, that would be:

Profit (money earned) = Selling Price (what you will sell it for) – (**minus**) Cost Price (what you paid to buy the stock):

So, let's say you buy a box of candy for $7 and the usual selling price is $20, that's one huge profit already as long as you stick to the usual selling price.

$13.00 profit = $20.00 - $7.00

To look in more detail, the box of candies cost $7.00 and it came with 20 individually wrapped candies. If you sold each candy for $1.00, in the end, you'll have made a total of $20.00 and yet you only spent $7 buying them.

The difference in the two prices is your earnings or profit.

Cost price of a candy box with 20 candies in: $7.00

Selling price per piece of candy: $1.00

Amount sold: 20 x $1.00 = $20

Profit: $20.00 - $7.00 = $13

To really think like a mogul kid, you now have $13 extra dollars in your hand and have to decide what to do with that.

A real mogul kid would take $7.00 out of the $20.00 dollars again and buy another box of candy. The leftover $13.00 is to be placed in your piggy bank because that's what you worked hard for. Keep it to spend later. Repeat this cycle to grow your profit in your business. So, every time you sell a box—or twenty individual candies—to your friends and neighbors, you will have $13.00 to put in your piggy bank as your profit and you'll be able to buy another box of candies.

Even better, if the stockist you keep buying candies from sees that you're a regular buyer, he may agree to sell to you for a little less than you paid the last time, especially if you can buy more than one box. And can you even think of a way to make the profit even bigger? Have a guess…

That's right: make your own candies! Go to the library or find a book online on Amazon; most books let you read X number of pages for free, and if you do your research well, you will find candy recipes you can follow yourself, with your parents' help and permission to use the cooker safely.

This way, you'll buy your ingredients—like sugar, colorants, flavorings—online and use a little on gas and electricity, before producing home-made candies that can be even more appealing to buyers, and so earn a high profit.

The better you do your business research, the more interesting your business 'hobby' will become! And the more profit you'll make.

**

Another type of business to think about is assisting a family member at work.

Assisting on the Job

Have you ever thought about helping a family member who already has a specialty? A specialty is described as a job they can do very well. Their specialty is more of a hobby to them and it allows them to spend their time doing it while it benefits them by helping them to support their family.

You may have a relative who has a lawn business, a carpentry business, carpet-cleaning business, a mobile pet-grooming business or a beautician business. You can easily ask your family member if you can work with them to get paid on the weekends.

If your relative has a lawn service, pick up papers and bottles in the yard being serviced, or rake up clippings and leaves, or water the flowers. Or, if your relative is a barber and has a barber shop, you can work there to offer the clients water bottles, charge their phones when asked, make drinks or to sweep the barbershop.

All you are showing everyone is that you are willing to work and earn money for personal savings.

One word of warning, though: be careful in the work you do, even if someone asks you to do it. They may not be aware of the risks involved—especially if they did that same job as a young person and the laws have changed—or of the legal restrictions on what young workers can be employed to do. You do not want to get hurt or land your relative in trouble.

Just be sensible is all.

For example, in the beautician's salon, do sweep the floor and tidy up, but do not handle dangerous chemicals like dyes or acids.

Make cold drinks but not teas and coffees as you may scald yourself or someone else.

In the gardening company, do pick up litter (always wear work gloves!), water the flowers and trees, pick up clippings—but never operate any machine, not even a lawn mower.

And in a doggy daycare business, do walk the dog in a safe, fenced area but not roaming free in public spaces since if anything happened—like a dog escaped and hurt someone—your employer would be liable. Also, do feed the dogs but do not agree to give medication. You get the idea, right?

Take on only the safe and simple tasks until you're legally old enough to do the more responsible ones.

But you'll soon see, to earn money has no age limit or major restrictions. You have to be willing to put time into your work to earn the money you want. To become a mogul kid, you must probably spend your weekends working quite hard or you will not increase your money like you want. If your family owns a restaurant, you can ask them if you can be hired to help fill the soda machines, or stock the bags, spoons, fork and knives for a *little fee*. Yes, I said little fee because when you are asking to help, you have to remain humble. Plus, you may not be very useful at all in the beginning! Expect to feel like you're not very good at the job, and that you get under everyone's feet. So, ask for a small amount of pay and then that gives you a reason to request a pay raise when they find they can't get by without you!

Always keep the mindset of a mogul kid; thinking of a little fee for work will someday help you to own your own business in no time. Remember, if you start to devote your time into earning money now as a kid and you start to save, you will become that mogul kid that eventually transforms into a mogul adult.

Reading

If you do not want to sell candy in school, think of a skill or hobby to do after school or on weekends. As an example, if you love to read, find out if there are little children aged 2 to 5 to whom you can read and charge their parents. You can also help them with their homework.

You can have your parents help you create a flyer to advertise in your neighborhood that you do story time with children in that age group for one hour at your house or the nearest library for $5 a week, Monday through Friday. (be careful not to go into strangers' homes. They must come to you so your parents can be sure they are good, responsible people).

Another suggestion is to ask the library nearest your house if you can come on Saturdays at a certain time and read to the younger children for one hour and charge $1 per child. That is a positive move for you as a child and the library nearest you to provide reading time for $1 per child. In this case, you can make $10 if you have 10 children or $15 if you have 15 children.

And imagine what this might do to your future career if, say, you want to be a support worker, a crèche or youth worker or a teacher! Wow! You just got your adult working life off to a great start by being able to put this onto your work history—and with a reference from the library.

At the end of your reading time, you can take your money home and place it in a piggy bank so you can continue saving. Saving your money will help your business grow to the extent that one day, you won't have to grow it anymore.

Remember, you are choosing to do something that interests you for you to make fun but honest money. The mogul child who is making money for doing what she/he loves is expanding day by day. Becoming a business child is not difficult; you just have to find what you like to do. That one thing you like to do is that particular business you can start to have. There are plenty of job options for children to become successful mogul children.

Being Creative

In addition, if you have any computer skills, you can make money for your knowledge. To think more creatively as a tycoon, you have to be imaginative. If you are familiar with the computer system, create and print personalized bookmarks and put encouraging quotes on them to sell. You can use funny quotes like, *Get off your phone and continue reading,* or *Do not answer your phone call in the middle of reading.* Or, *Yes, Facebook will still be there later!* Or even, *I'd rather be on Facebook.*

The ideas I am giving are for you to become the successful mogul kid I am training you to be.

In being creative, you must be original. Being original is what makes you stand out which will result in your business growing. You can list a couple of funny quotes on the bookmarks and print them and have your parent laminate them for you—or do that yourself too, with the right training. The bookmarks are unique because my children's friends became intrigue and frequently asked my children about them. What about getting a hold of your friends' and their parents' photos and putting these into laminated bookmarks too? Wouldn't that be great! Now, you can sell to kids and to parents alike—double the market!

You can sell the bookmarks $1-$2 each in school, at the library, or in front of a grocery store. This type of creative business is cost effective because the Microsoft program comes with eight bookmarks on one sheet. All you have to do is type the information into the bookmark and put your business name at the bottom.

You can make some in color or some in black and white and then save and print. Afterwards, you can laminate and cut them. If you sell each bookmark for $1, you will make $8 per page. On the other hand, if you sell each bookmark for $2, you will make $16 per printed page.

There are many things listed in the word document gallery that you can choose from to create your own business idea. Remember, you have to be creative so your business can earn you some money.

Once again, the main focus of making money is doing what interests you so you wouldn't want to stop. The many purpose of becoming a mogul kid is being a kid that makes money while having fun.

Special Skills

Have you discovered your special talent? All children and adults have a special talent unique to them. Another suggestion you can implement into your life to make money is sharing your talent.

To share your talent, all you have to do is choose a busy location where people are seen going in and out. Choosing a busy location like a grocery store, nursing home, hospital lobby, the mall, or a storefront can really help you gain a large profit. All you have to do is ask the business if it's alright for you to share your talent with the community at their location on a weekly basis.

Make sure to let the business know what day and time is convenient for you. Whatever you are talented in, like dancing, singing, or playing an instrument, it can be performed at a business place. Place a donation box in front of you while exercising your performance. With these types of skills, you can make more money because people usually donate more money to children who show interest in a certain specialty. And here's a tip: grandparents *love* to tip kids, because seeing you do what you're good at brings them joy! So, where can you perform in front of old people? Not only are you having fun, but they are too! Oh, and no matter what you are doing, always thank every person who places an amount in your tray.

Conclusion

Your originality can so easily become a profitable business venture so keep looking for ways to grow, and don't lose heart; determination and keeping on repeating the same thing you love will make you an expert at it. And everyone loves to see a kid who's an expert at something.

A mogul person also doesn't just look for one way to make money; they may look for several ways, just because that is what mogul people do. But don't move into a second area until you're a whizz-kid at the first, since you're just diluting your time and energy.

Summary

Making Dollars Make Sense: Business Ownership at any Age is a powerful little guide for children with an ambitious mission to teach every child timeless financial advice that will give them a head start in life.

This nifty little guide will teach children the importance of financial independence and the skills needed to be able to handle money properly at a young age, as well as instilling in them the adventurous spirit of entrepreneurship.

This book will also teach your kids to see opportunity for earning a little income everywhere and shift their mindsets from seeing their parents or guardians as the only source of income, to relying on themselves.

C. PIERRE-RUSSELL

 was born and raised in sunny Miami, FL, it was natural for Cheurlie Pierre-Russell to join the United States Navy.

Her high point came during Operation Uphold Democracy on the island nation of Haiti, where she worked as a translator. Leaving the Navy was difficult but it was time to start a family and tackle a new career.

C. Pierre-Russell graduated from Georgia State University with a Bachelor of Arts in Sociology, later earning a Master of Science in Psychology from Walden University.

Her desire to strive in education led her to study the development and perception of children's lives through the influence of social context, and she has also studied children's intellectual development.

These combined areas of interest influenced her to write children's books, to help them understand their own cognitive way of life.

A strong role model for women and children, C. Pierre-Russell is a wife and has three amazing children of her own.

Now, she writes both fiction and non-fiction for kids of all ages, covering many subjects.

C. Pierre-Russell feels every child is a future leader and deserves only the best!

To find out about C. Pierre-Russell's next book release,
visit her Instagram page: https://www.instagram.com/j3russellbook/
or her Facebook page: https://www.facebook.com/

www.ingramcontent.com/pod-product-compliance
Lightning Source LLC
Chambersburg PA
CBHW051604010526
44118CB00023B/2812